The Milk of Your Blood

The Milk of Your Blood

A Collection of Poems

José Luís Oseguera

Cover design by Shay Culligan:

ISBN: 978-1-950462-92-6

Kelsay Books Inc.

kelsaybooks.com

502 S 1040 E, A119
American Fork,Utah 84003

*for my wife, Nicole,
and my son, Gio*

Acknowledgments

Grateful acknowledgment is made to the editors of the following journals and anthologies in which these poems or earlier versions of them appeared.

Anthropocene: "Chinga tu Madre"
Anthropocene: "Pacts with the Devil"
Anthropocene: "Reseda Boulevard"
The Bangalore Review: "In the City of Panorama"
The Basil O'Flaherty: "Red as a Rose Was She"
Burningword Literary Journal: "Being Able To"
Castabout Art & Literature: "Sur Place du Petit-Point"
Cathexis Northwest Press: "My heart is a headless pigeon"
Duck Lake Journal: "Psaume Framboise"
The Esthetic Apostle: "Luceros"
The Inquisitive Eater: "Till Death Do Us Part"
Heirlock Magazine: "Topanga Canyon"
Hiram Poetry Review: "Tiller of the Ground"
Leaping Clear: "In the Light of the Bas-Relief"
Leaping Clear: "The Opossum"
Meat for Tea: "Hijo de Puta"
Meat for Tea: "Whole"
Noctua Review: "In Ramah"
The Northridge Review: "The Milk of Your Blood"
The Olivetree Review: "Ode to a Single Mother of Three from Three Different Men"
Open Arts Forum: "The House on Tilden Avenue"
The Piltdown Review: "Calanques"
The Piltdown Review: "Du Monde"
The Piltdown Review: "Super Mario Bros. Coin"
Sky Island Journal: "Hija de Hombre"
Sky Island Journal: "In the Shadow of the Drowning Mammoth"

Sky Island Journal: "The flicker of her eyes"
Streetlight Magazine: "Ferning"
The Write Launch: "A Grimoire Ajar"
The Write Launch: "Moving Day"

My deepest gratitude to Daniel Overberger, Voltaire Tiñana, Cory Bilicko, Winnie Ocean, Allan Smorra, Jason Taksony Hewitt, Judith Estanislao Campbell, Lindsay Armstrong Vance, Adam Bowling, Steve Martin, Lina Ogolla, Vivian Taslakian, Julie and Karen Kelsay, Shay Culligan and the Kelsay Books team, my teachers, Mom and Paul, Pedro and Nadia, Dad, Joe and Rita Gyomber, my family, friends and WordPress followers.

In loving memory of Soledad and Pedro Ramírez.

Contents

Milk

In Ramah

Mexicans don't believe in miscarriages;
they believe in *angelitos*—
when you die in the womb,
you're born in heaven.

Mom lost a *criaturita*
four months before she found out
that she was pregnant with me,
which—if I'm doing the math right—
was 2 months before she married Dad.

I was born overtime, in September 1985—
a 10-pound fetus of 10 months—
which puts my date of conception
around Dad's 18th birthday.

"Scorpios always get their way,"
my brother often said.
"And Geminis give it up fast.
They have two faces:
una de santita y la otra de putita."

At the OB/GYN,
Mom had to declare prior pregnancies
that ended in termination:
whether by choice through abortion—
a sin beyond the grasp of evil—

or by God's will through miscarriage,
because He wasn't bad,
and she was the one to blame,
she was no good as a woman:
"What are we if not to birth?" Mom would say.

As the stinky cotija cheese we hid under
the passenger seat of Dad's '93 royal-blue Corsica
whenever the Tijuana-San Diego border patrol stared
at our yellowing birth certificates a little too long—
wondering if they were real—

and asked if we were sure
there were *really* only 5 people in the car,
Mom would struggle to smuggle in her mouth
the very real child she'd lost over 10 years before,
one whose body continued to grow
heavy on her mind, wondering:
what would've he looked like by now?

It was a truth she kept on her tongue,
and never dared swallow
so that her first baby knew
we hadn't forgotten about him.

In our house, we were always a family of 6,
before Dad went to jail for the last time,
because the boy that wasn't—
he who didn't spill Mom's placenta

like chicken soup foaming
over the pot's embrace,
hissing off the fire,
soaking the dirty ground—

he who had no name,
would've fathered her grandchildren:
a voiceless thought that would never
call her *Mamá.*

Hija de Hombre

Grandma would always smack the nail clippers
from Mom's hand whenever she tried to cut my infant toenails,
out of fear that it would cause me blindness.

Yet, she lied to her daughter—
locked in the bathroom—
about baptizing me
in the name of the Father,
the Son and the Holy Ghost
in the yellowed-pink vanity,

dousing my wrinkled forehead
with a methodically-knobbed
current of hot and cold,
waving a three-fingered St. Andrew's cross—
patron saint of fishermen,
fishers of men and women who threw them back in—
under the calcium-green faucet
over Mom's shouts of *Open the door and let me in!:*
"May Christ's words be on his mind,
on his lips, and in his heart."

Never to be like the man
who married her daughter at the altar
and burned her at the stake.

Pounding the recycled wood
with the residual anger Mom never got to
release on Dad's chest begging him to tell her
a truth she didn't want to believe
once she heard it.

Mom wanted to stop Grandma's magical faith
in God's wonder-working power
because she knew that the power of her own blood—
running in me, side-by-side with his—
didn't need another man,
real or ethereal,
to help her raise the boy
she and she alone
grew from within herself.

Mom's breasts—small, unassuming,
rich in unperishable milk
seasoned of rosewater, mint, and honey,
enough to feed their baby,
not calm his desire for another's—
nestled my soaking head
and dried it warm with the long hair
she braided together as the Euphrates did
the Pishon, Gihon, and Tigris,
from Eden to me.

It was a lone rosary—
hexed as it was hallowed—
that slithered down her spine
between her haloed shoulders,
untouched by a man's deceiving palms:
kisses that continued to warm,
words that burned her back dimples.

How she dreaded from minute one
as I cried bloody—
defenseless on her flower-patterned hospital gown—
the last breath I'd breathe into my child-being
and exhale into the breadth of manhood:
the day I'd cease to be hers and become my own.

"You would've made such a pretty girl," she'd tell me
as apples reddened on my cheeks,
hanging from a tree whose thick roots
and heavy boughs shattered its nursery pot.

She harped Grandma's silver-clouded tresses
to the tune of her raspy, voiceless hums,
a song stuck in her throat
from days when her hair rippled raven-black
in the drafty church, as her daughter
drew houses in the prayer books,
where she lashed out, in silence, at Christ's crucified body
for her *niña* to be healed
of the darkness that hid men's true nature
from the women who loved them.

She allowed Mom to trim it so short
just to show her that the sweet sound
of God's amazing grace not only
healed the blind, but revealed that
fiddling with things that cut
was a young woman's stupidity.

Hijo de Puta

A bloody nose
because no matter how many
oil changes stained her elbows
or broken windows scarred her hands,
she wasn't man enough to be a father—
they hated you because she still loved him.

Its viscosity dripped from your upper lip
smeared on your T-shirt sleeve like a mischief of rats
dispersing to light switched on,
embarrassed red as if it knew
that Mom could only bleach away the stains
not Dad's absence festering in your veins.

The bootleg Dodgers cap that hid your giant forehead
and brow horns reminded their fists of him—
they beat you because he beat her—
laughing as they had their fun, knuckling the
the whirlpool of hair
you failed to quell with petroleum jelly, night after night;
the mousy cowlick you definitely got
from his side of the family, not theirs.

A body as protection,
mutilated by eyes that only saw fat—
starving itself to starve them of words—
you learned to nourish the skinny boy
in the bathroom mirror by gliding
your fingers in his rib hollows:
the grooves of the chest where you hid yourself.

Night sanded, primed,
and lacquered scratches and dents
the day bruised had on her body,
your home.

Her frown as warm as the stew
she left on the stove for you
to throw away the next day.

Ode to a Single Mother of Three from Three Different Men

She had to carry the world,
and that of her children,
on a back condemned only
to suffer the weight of two breasts.

Pinche puta was the nickname
her parents, siblings, and church members
fashioned for her
out of murmurs, throat-clears and avoided eye contact.

Men loved her for making them feel like men,
for giving them children so that they'd stay,
and the freedom to abandon her and her other children—
also from fathers who didn't want them—
whenever they felt the urge to find themselves another *pendeja.*

Sex was forbidden when her uncle gagged her little mouth,
holy when she married the dad of her oldest at 16,
forgiven when the dad of her youngest started fucking her cousin,
sinful when she fucked his brother:

it was a weapon to fight, not for love,
for stability, gambling with her desire,
wagering her fertility and waging war with
another man lost—another son birthed—
only to see if she'd win this time.

Tiller of the Ground

My brother didn't ask for my mother's womb
to open its mouth to receive her husband's seed.
He didn't ask to be part of a family sapling
too diseased to be called a marriage.

He didn't ask to live in an apartment building
where the property manager's kids acted
as their mother's henchmen—
garnering fear from the kids

who slept cramped
on hand-me-down mattresses
as she garnished their parents' Welfare checks—
because she was jealous

of how torrid and impetuous and dashing
her "assistant" manager husband
wore his grin whenever Mom needed something fixed—
then 26 and mostly single.

He wasn't at fault
for his mother's beauty and selfishness—
an abandoned, immigrant woman starved
for the kindness and warmth and lies

of any man stupid enough to harvest
the fruit of his vigor for her pale,
brunette, wild honey—tender as lush as foreplay—
miraging as clear as forbidden sex.

He didn't ask to read the letters Dad
sent from prison, written in false promises
on paper made of the pulped bark,
inner flesh of stumps pruned dead.

He didn't ask to be too young
to understand rejection and disappointment
from someone who had become so good
at hiding them in her impatience and chagrin—

our comfort, craving for the heat of her violence;
a woman whom I questioned in silence,
while she distracted herself with absence,
whether she was really a mother

or someone pretending to be one
because she was stuck in a prison
which bound her to us in a way
that correctional bars set her husband free.

He didn't ask for his wailing kindergarten body—
still soft and fuzzy of baby hair—
to be soil for the manager's kids to till,
their whaling fists stripped from my sinews

his little spirit which wasn't fully formed—
the layers between skin and muscle,
bone and soul, blood and breath—
cried to me, buried in their laughter.

He didn't ask to be born two years after
my empty trunk, shaking as it petrified,
when my hands twinged as twigs—my shoes as roots—
because they were filled with rage as a tree with sap.

He didn't ask for his eyes
to be so large that he couldn't hide anything,
melting as the older of the two Cains
held his arms back, sternum up—

a loser before I had the courage to face his sacrifice—
while the smaller kid punched my boy, my son by omission:
it was a matter of honor,
something you defended when all else was lost.

The leaves on the trees—
falling before it was their turn—
paved our way back home
in summer's heat, when the days were longer

and the dads came home
tired, dirty, hungry, empty-handed
without a dad to give us,
as if they'd lost him somewhere along the way.

Being Able To

or

(A Letter to My Brother I Wrote, Ripped, and Retaped)

Real men should be afraid of nothing,
especially not of other men.
But what of those they don't consider to be real men?
What about the fear of even touching their blood
because it probably has AIDS?
The fear that makes every son a blessing;
every gay son a curse:
a death in the family,
a non-existent thing,
a vanishing.

Faggot for allowing your heart to decide.
Faggot for letting your back arch
like a dog in heat for another man to make you his.
Faggot for breaking your mother's heart,
and her father's father's,
and his Father who is in heaven:
hallowed be His name,
hollowed was yours on her lips
when she used to ring your wrists
until your 6-year-old hands went numb,
as she yelled into your big brown eyes,
and wished that you were more like me.
Your place in the afterlife hijacked
by one who loves women
just like he's supposed to,
and takes it without complaining:

because prayer can fix anything—
like Vicks VapoRub and Robitussin—
because *Don't worry it'll pass*

will also pass, and you will be judged
by people who call themselves family,
who hate you because you're not what they
think a man should be:
what your Creator made you as
when He made *you* the way He made you.
He loves you and—along with all the angels
in eternity—is cheering for you
to grab your piece of heaven by force.

And rather than queer the hell
they used to torture you with,
I joined in willingly because I didn't know any better,
because I'd rather be wrong than be your brother,
because protecting you meant making myself weak.

Back when I wasn't strong enough to be strong for you too,
you were stronger for the both of us,
and all of those who needed to form a mob
in order to be strong against you.

I wanted to protect you from yourself
and all the evil in your veins—
the meth in your madness—
when you told me you were HIV positive,
how I wished for you to be 6 again
so that I could finally be stronger than you,
and wrap you in my arms against your will
until you cried yourself to sleep;
I'd carry you to your room
and heal your wounds with my kisses.

But even in your weakened state,
you wouldn't have needed my help
the way the phoenix doesn't
need a firefighter to aid it
as its heart burns to ash,
or a sculptor to fashion
its feathers anew from cinder.

There will always be men who will hate you
just to make themselves feel like men,
as they preach the Gospel of Jesus—love incarnate—
and hide in His bleeding lashes their fear of faggots,
killing Abel—the world's first gay man and martyr—
time and time again, out of jealousy,
because God loved him more.

In the City of Panorama

some trees are male, some female;
our house had four of them,
and though I circled them every day as a kid—
looking for any protrusions, danglings or slits—
I could never muster the courage
to ask Dad or Mom,
let alone the tree itself:
"Are you a man or a woman?"

Between the sweet gum—
where the June bugs clung
and hovered down gracefully
like fairies onto the dusty screen door
I once knifed near the handle at night
so that I could sneak back into the house
without disturbing the fallen
seed pods, sharp, sneezed across in the yard,
great ammunition to play fight,
aiming for exposed skin,
to hurt each other for a laugh,
never to wound,
practicing for our turn to join
the game our parents were so good at—

and the avocado tree—
whose bird-pecked fruit dangled rotten
until winds beyond us slapped them loose,
plunged to their guacamole death,
thuds on the roof in the early morning
like a giftless Santa Claus
in the dead of summer
when Dad's mistress,
"*only* a friend," as he referred to her,
wore midriff Led Zeppelin T-shirts

and demanded to be more than his wife,
as she rammed her car into ours
two hours late to school
until he got fed up with her torrid love,
got out of the car and cracked her jaw
as easily as the pits expelled
from the avocados' bellies,
seamless in its violence
as a couple blinded by desire
and the loathing that mashed lust into love:
he hated her more
than I'd ever seen him hate Mom,
and that was the real reason
why she hated his girlfriend too.

The olive—
who never once believed
that my short life was far more
contorted than its deformed
branches and elephant skin,
but it soon understood why Dad
would rather party with his girlfriend
than sleep in the same bed as Mom
a room away from ours,
where he was supposed to rest
like an ax behind glass for when nightmares came
a simple shatter could bring about
its strong grip to warm your hands,
rather than the chill it hacked down my spine.
Its sun-tanned berries—
regurgitated skins and pits on the asphalt—
exposed the tires percussive
rolling down the driveway in neutral,
his breath geared low, aware that whatever it was

that he was leaving to do
wasn't because he loved us—

and sweet pittosporum tree—
whose fallen leaves lay on the grass,
disgraced stars from nights before,
laughed with me like pork rinds crackling in oil
attempting a sneak attack on my little sister,
its sticky seed ovaries fell
broken on the windshield
of Mom's silver Toyota—
Dad's car in his mind—
whose windows she pounded
as the weight of her tears
hung heavy knowing that
when you begged somebody to take you back,
you did it out of pain,
not out of love.

By the time I came to know what sex was
and love had bloomed and died
deep inside my trunk,
I realized that all the trees
shading our house growing up
must've been female
because, like Mom, they all stayed rooted in their place
the day that he left us.

Chinga tu Madre
or
(Things That Didn't Turn Out Quite as Planned)

Because her love hurt
as that of a lioness
sinking her canines
into her cubs' soft skulls—
devouring each one,
not out of hunger or hatred
but compassion and love—

she tortured and killed
all of the men—
the wilderness budding within,
Eden blooming poisoned apple blossoms—
she didn't want me to ripen into.

Whenever their corpses
pulled my child wrists—
diseased fingers cupping boyish upspeak—
she'd flog my soft flesh
with bare hand to redden,
reshape the human plasticine
churned from within herself
as rotting blood from an exit wound
into someone unlike her,
something that wasn't Dad,
somewhere distant from myself.

"A good father can't come
from a good father,"
she used to say.
"Just as spilling an exceptional vintage on dirt
will not yield good wine grapes."

In her mind, hoarding such an abundance
of decency by the few men whose fathers slept
in the same bed as their wives was needless carnage:
house-broken males who felt instant remorse
when they lost their temper,
ate meals prepared by their work-ladened hands,
and locked themselves in the bathroom
with a newspaper, not porn, for hours at a time.

It never mattered if Mom loved Dad or not,
that he was glad to be or not to be the father,
or if he was disappointed that she never thought
of him as "daddy" material:
pregnancy does not birth a mother from a woman,
as having unprotected sex
spurt a father from a man.

What is a mother
if not one who nurses you
even though she hates
that your breathing reminds her
of the blood knot that binds her to him—
destroyer of lives lived and unlived—
for a lifetime divorced
of the vows they once wedded;
the one who loves you
not because you're hers to mind
but in spite of it.

Everyone in the history of everything
wouldn't care enough to submerge their claws
into my flesh, and rip away until tears
rolled down both our faces—
unafraid of the spatter,

memories of the woman who chose love,
but whom love never chose back—
and all that remained of us
was a shell of her,
the ghost of him,
and the nothingness of me.

Red as a Rose Was She

She rose in early morning, the day
of new hope—spring in January—
as the sun thawed her heart
blossoming red once more.

The silk of a man's tenderness
lost in her rent memories of a husband—
bruised petals at his feet—
and a youth he strew about
wildly as if love were a trinket to torture her with—
violence on her scars.

Years plot in bad soil, her rose wilted,
waiting for no one, as she allowed her beauty
to shame from the light:
falling backwards into his empty embrace,
gouging the double-edged thorns of his promise blind,
learning that mistakes can't teach you a thing
until you make them;
and even so, you make them again and again.

The blood she shed in tears and petals withered—
notwithstanding the love he husbanded—
rid her of the flower befuddled by masculinity,
the one who used to palm grit aimlessly
for romance's indecipherable leaves:
the charm of his eyes,
the vow of his smile,
the succor of his virility.
She sifted through all the tarnish
not for what love had deprived her of;
but rather, for what it still owed her.

We watched her walk down the aisle
as if we saw her, but witnessed
what she no longer was.
Miraculously—as dead as plucked on asphalt,
arid by the everyday—
at its core, the bud entombed in petals
ever so crimson fluttered on her cheeks,
and bled love anew on the day of her wedding.

The House on Tilden Avenue

was a pair of trousers
with five pockets;
strewn, wrinkled, gouged
empty when Mom first told us
she was leaving it
to live with her new husband—
her third boyfriend ever.

I felt guilty for feeling nothing
when she called yelling at me
to come pick up all of the shit
I didn't need to carry anymore.
It was the stuff she asked me to hold
while she nailed family portraits on walls of sand
and she'd ask me to wear the pants
that reminded her of Dad
whenever she needed someone to fight with;
her tears, and his absence,
always melted them away.

The grudge weighed heavy still on her shoulders
even after she gave the landlord all of Dad's bullets,
my uncle, all of his 90's porno VHS tapes,
and Goodwill, all of the furniture he'd collected—
discarded by other families—
to furnish neither the house he never bought her,

nor the abandoned the shell we no longer wanted:
these worthless quarters,
hearth blackened beyond use;
a mother within a wife within a woman
who looked sad even when she smiled.

At that elementary age, I always wondered
if things would've been easier for her if I had died in my sleep.
On long, summer nights when she went to bed,
I would closed my eyes
and I pray for food, and a Dad,
and ask God to forgive me for Mom having neither,
for not praying hard enough
because why would He forsake
the people who saved what little they had
when hope was all that was left
in our tepid refrigerator and in Mom's paycheck—
nothing accumulated, everything lost.

How empty and small it looked
and how naked I felt standing there
when I returned to see what was left of me;
what was left to remember of what we had forgotten.
All I found was the scent of linden tea,
Mom's drink of choice when she was alone.

The problem wasn't that I never liked the house,
even when we first moved in
and it smelled of fresh paint and carpet,
walls white and smooth before Dad
started bruising his hands through them,

or that I hated it because it was haunted
by our dead selves—
the hiding, the shame, the lack of warmth,
the bonemeal of nostalgia
floating as fibers in the evening sun,
without the violence, without the pain
to make us a family strong again;
the problem was that she had made it her home.

Du Monde

"Who won?" Mom texted.
Mexico was playing Brazil
in the World Cup's last of 16:
I didn't have the heart to reply.

Why didn't she take his hand,
the guy from São Paulo
she often spoke about—
as we commiserated with Cinderella on VHS
in our one-bedroom apartment—
too little even for two—
hungry, sleepy, aged 28, 6, 7,
and 9 at 10:36 p.m.,
waiting for the man she married
to finally transform into Prince Charming?

He was nothing like the one whom she told
she didn't like to dance
even though she wanted to kiss him
and described his nose, jaw, and eyebrows
so well that my eyes grew misty
breathing the spiced rum in his breath,
the scent of his musk and sweat beading on his chest.

That night, she tapped her feet
alone at the party,
and under her silk sheets
wiggling her toes warm.
Instead, she fell for a man
from her native Mexico—

bronze skin, thin body,
and honeyed-milk promises—
who made it a habit of stealing her car
and leaving their kids at school
until cleaning ladies from Michoacán—
generous enough to palm their grey uniforms
for coins to give them
to buy chips and soda—
had to kick them out
into the street to eat on the sidewalk,
the curb as their chair and table.

When my phone buzzed again,
raring to be given the pleasure of letting Mom down,
I wanted to thumb "I don't know,"
just as I would've wanted Dad
to present Mom with her missing glass slipper.

"Brazil," I finally replied.
A phantom ellipsis palpitated incessantly
on my screen for five minutes—
an eternity ever after.
I checked back after 45:
she hadn't replied.

My heart is a headless pigeon

roosting desiccated on a road
trudged by my grandparents
from Michoacán to Los Angeles;
it thrashes as a facedown newborn
begging to be picked up
and nurtured with seed on my chest.

"Look, I think his eyes are going to be blue,"
Mom said, as if her incessant repetition—
a trapped bird trying to fly through glass—
would make the recessive pigment
in her half-Mexican, half-White grandchild's eyes
congeal like a yolk at the center of his whites.

"But as cute and *güero* as you see him," she warned,
"he is filled with sin, and it's your job to hit him
so that he grows up to be happy and healthy."
Although a grandchild was all
she wanted ever since she found semen-stained
tighty-whities in my laundry hamper when I was twelve.
Mom didn't mind clipping her grandchild's wings
so long as it saved his soul,
tarring him with her Savior's blood,
feathering his path with her knowledge of good and evil—
my love pecked by her hate,
my dove shooed away like a common street pigeon
by her rolled-up version of Truth.

Little did Mom know that there had been a little bird—
of my wattle and her feather—
that never got to hatch,
whose downy fuzz never met the wind,
hungry beak never swallowed feed from its mother's own,
and whose birdsong went unsung and unheard;
a baby who had survived only in my mind, not in memory.

She looked at her *nieto* proudly—
his stare, empty iris and nothing more—
and then at the TV, Spanish news
reporting on a man who'd been
decapitated and electrocuted
on power lines—somewhere in El Salvador—
attempting to save two children
stuck on a neighbor's roof, feeding bread to the birds.

When the foul scent of seedy poop
and spoiled mother's milk overtook the newborn smell,
Mom shoved my son's wiggly body towards me—
intermittently stiff and limp with chirps and coos—
as if it were a featherless baby bird
fallen from a tree that she wanted me to throw away;
he flapped his tiny wing arms,
batting tiny lashes over unfocused eyes
that cried but couldn't yet shed a single tear
for himself or for his lost sibling,
one whose shell broke too soon
and left my heart spangled with its shards,
wet with my blood that would've been hers.

Even so, my prayers for her empty bones
won't put to flight the spilled yoke before me,
heaving as red as prey ready
for the crows and vultures
of Mom's rights and wrongs to raven;
their razor talons unaware
of my child's microscopic heart still beating in mine.

Blood

Psaume Framboise

You had horns
when I first met you,
and your laughter echoed
as bleats ramming

against all of my hard parts—
the walls I built
to protect myself from
ever being trampled by love again.

Your absent-minded gaze
twisted into me as sharpened bone,
a gore deeper than the sheepish dimples that formed
atop your cheeks as apples with missing stems.

You gazed at me without seeing
the wound bleeding from a body
grazed down to barely human by divorce—
more cattle than man,

cursed with the heart of a lover
the size of a human head,
utterly disappointed by what had become
of the milk it could no longer express.

I was content with not knowing where you
had slept the night before—
where you were coming from
or where you were going—

but your description of how you'd once deflowered
a guy 5 years older than you
stampeded my guts thrilled.

Or how you always had male friends who wanted to fuck
but you hung out with them anyway,
and bored through their bareback melodies—
hearts broken like porcelain—
as they clung unto your hugging them goodbye.

Goat-eyed honeydew I stared
as we walked side by side
down a long, rectangular hallway.
Your voice startled me;
it was foolishly married to joy
as I was to horniness's empty embrace.

I ventured into your unknown,
not to lose myself but to be found;
I chased you not to cage you,
but to be shepherded into a constellation
of grass blades that glimmered with dew,
individually brushstroked by young bees
with their virgin honey.

You were wild, you were free,
you didn't style your hair the same
color for more than a month,
and goaded me by calling yourself
a *galletita fuerte*—tough cookie in the bad Spanish
you wanted me to help you with
my mediocre *pocho-Spanglish.*

Even if I'd seen you kissing another
in a dark corner of that same building,
I'd simply shake my head, yet never stride away:
you were *my* lover,

46

and I wasn't going to be afraid
to walk up to you and run
my hands through your hair,
feel your antlers and the sharp
that had yet to reveal itself under it all.

A Grimoire Ajar

A candle is lit.
Its pink flesh melts smooth at first,
but as its silk ribbons
cascade from its frozen bluffs,
it withers as its wick slowly
bores deep into its heart.

It's made of a wax that floods
the cracks in the earth
deep within me, like hindmilk,
where my soul first took root.

Its viscosity flowed as wasteful as time,
until a mold hidden
in a stranger's smile
brought about a sleepless night
blanketed in Schubert's
Die liebe Farbe on loop.

Its molten core began to harden
as she took me in her arms
and made me a shelter
with the scent of her soft palate,
the vapor condensing on her chest—
balmy on my stubbled chin—
her upper lip fevered
red at an ember's pace,
all tasted of coconut water,
dulce de leche and blood-saliva.

There were many moons waxing that night
in alien worlds as deprived of oxygen
as the space between our tongues—
orbiting in harmony—

but the moon hiding bright
behind the cypresses
would remain forever nameless
as the gasps for air
she stole from me.

Mein Schatz hat's Grün so gern
haloed over our consumed bodies
as in the cartoons whenever
a bludgeoned fool lay flat, overtaken
by a force greater than himself.

She nestled into the soft thicket
between my armpit and chest—
a crater that gleamed in her absence.
But even as she palmed the gritty, cold linoleum
off her brindled-leather motorcycle boots,
the mold had closed,
the wax had set:
blow out the candle,
breathe in the ashen smoke.

Reseda Boulevard

Strewn bedsheets cast a mold of your hips,
my eyes dazzled by the lights you flicked off,
the scent of your equator
guided my famished lips
to the vast land that separates
your breasts from your navel;
it filled the space behind my heart—
between my throat and spine—
with the heat of your eyes
as smoke from a wood fire
bathed by a drizzle on summer dirt.

The inner flesh of your thighs—
curtains made of caramelized velvet—
muffled the sound of your pleasure writhings,
yet amplified the underwater flutters
of my tongue swimming in your labia—
sharp and sweet as bruised ginger.

They were as waves of jitters
that come from unwrapping a present,
licking the frosted head off a cupcake—
a smile at the back of your mouth
when you realize a single sprinkle
wedged itself, secretly, in your molar crater
as your upper and lower teeth
jigsaw perfectly into one another.

The mattress stayed warm
as your trickles echoed in the toilet
and the strip of light under the bathroom door
awoke me from our dream.

After you removed your contacts
and washed your face, staring at the mirror
as if you'd never seen yourself in it before,
your hands twitched on the vanity
as in your piano finger exercises.

Before you entered our bed
and interlaced your hands and feet into mine asleep,
my eyes released their squint
from the time blinking red on your dresser;
it throbbed shadows on the empty cold
fabric that upholstered your side of the bed.

I drifted back to sleep with your taste
in my mouth: I palmed the strained metal springs—
unburdened still by your symmetry—
and they cried in silence,
hungry for the weight of your body.

The Milk of Your Blood

Evening sun pours its amber
into your eyes—fresh tea
that trickles into blue porcelain.
My fingers, plumes of steam,
bubblegum on the skin
around your nipple,
knit tightly as feather barbs—
turmeric and saffron in my throat.

In the eclipse of comforter and pillows,
my hums are shadows,
words, wind echoing in the quill
of what is left unsaid—
moths hide behind your earlobes
as the tarot of my lips dews the downy hairs
on the crucible nested between
your lower breast and false ribs—

it opens all the wounds
I collected like twine and twigs as a child
and ones you scattered over me
when I pecked your veins for seeds—
gooseflesh as scarred as rain thumbing the rubble,
ripping wings of tulip, poppy, and rose petals
strewn in your hair draped on the bed.

You penned a new gospel with my gasps—
the Holy Spirit dove crucified
with red plastic push pins
between your sinewy shoulder blades—
a Lord's Prayer that banished
my air, my ghost, my empty bones to dust.

The birds I raised in cages on the roof—
from speckled egg to flecked plumage—
breathed through your dry clothes wet
as they sung the music in your nose wrinkles.

Their beaks mocked the hocket on my puckered nape—
a warm cardamom breeze
fluttered the linen-white sheets
of the child smile that hid in adult teeth:
a halo mourning a ground hallowed;
the hollow we filled with home.

Topanga Canyon

My thumbs pushed cold
onto your warm, burnished obliques;
the other eight fingers
on your muscled back dimples.

You closed your eyes
and whatever it was that effervesced within you
settled and spumed out through
your gasps, visible smoke
in the bitter seabreeze.

Your breath escaped through the cracked windows
and clung to the spearmint sprigs—
the good herb, as it's known in Spanish—
it froze the flowers whiter
than white, a withered resonance
that didn't merely grab
the streetlight's piercing fluorescence;
it was light—eyes in the dark distance.

Your stomach had a mind of its own;
it convulsed, smiled and frowned,
dipping and billowing
as the sails of a ship lost in waves,
that would drown whomever dared cross it,

as when I took out a student loan
to buy tickets to Italy—
a trip we never took
because you wouldn't think of
crossing the Atlantic with someone
who hadn't said "I love you" first.

Your hips played a song
whose melody I'd never heard before
but whose verses I learned
as we used their pristine
flatness as clean canvas
to paint with the colors of my come.

By the time you needed to nestle
your cold body into mine,
I knew you from within an inch,
never to forget you from a mile.

Together, our bodies took on
the shape of steam;
nothing if not one.

The heat that left us
shipwrecked on the passenger seat's fabric
returned as the sun bathed the sea with light.

Pacts with the Devil

The house she dreamed about,
one that woke her up at night,
wasn't the one of her dreams—
Spanish style, Moorish tile,
on Highland Avenue
between 3rd and 6th street—

it was an old mansion
she'd first seen as a girl
with endless hallways
filled of creaks and shadows
and doors to rooms whose knobs
she dared not turn.

I told her about the summer—
between fourth and fifth grade—
in which I couldn't close my eyes
without hearing what I thought were
Satan's clip-clops at the foot of my bed,
as I wiped away her sweat
and stroked her dirty-blonde hair.

The only room she'd peeked into
huffed its door ajar;
it exhaled spider ash and pig breath,
wax images winked from its cobwebbed windows,
and smiled as long-lost sisters
whose laughter to play
called to her like cat chirrups.

The magic of swallowing a pill
wouldn't take effect for another three hours,
so we fell asleep
and I began to dream

about the town my grandma was born,
where witchcraft was the farmers'
only access to medical care,
even though the church forbade it.

According to Grandma, her grandfather would slash his palm
and shake the Devil's hand
to ensure that at least one
of his dodecatuplets survived birth:
his wife made it through,
but his twelve little apostles—
the midwife's nickname for his lost children—
did not; his blood was cursed, he died believing.

The house no one would ever inhabit
filled her mind once again
as her eyes woke up
spitting up tears, her throat full of vomit.
Her body was a home
but not for our little Messiah,
who was crucified
because of our sin.

We waited for night to come
so that we could sleep again,
but rest never came,
and the house that haunted her
grew larger with more rooms,
more questions, and one more ghost.
I held her as I released
what we had made,
the lie we had to make our truth:

someone had visited our little apartment home—
a little girl, because we had always wanted a little girl—
and though she couldn't stay to live with us,
I can still hear her footsteps at the side of my bed.

Till Death Do Us Part

There's the animal and its flesh.
At times interchangeable, but not quite the same.
Anglo-Saxon named the beasts, French their meat,
at death do they part:

beef from cow;
venison from deer; pork from pig;
mutton, sheep and poultry, chicken.
At what point does man become spouse?

Poussin is a young chicken, fowl good enough
to feed two young lovers, on not much money,
due to be wed in a few months,
not fully committed to a fully grown bird.

Poisson is fish, salmon we buy every other week
whenever we have extra cash
or need a breather from the chicken's—
butterflied in Ziploc bags—rotten egg smell:
"Throw it out and order a pizza"
is her solution to these odors of married life.

Pullet is a young hen.
"Pull it, and cut the wing off," I insist.
Even in my foul mood—
as our love grows old and the butter, brown—
I'm reminded of when I first loved her in the Tenderloin,
nested near the San Francisco Bay,
when the thought of being only hers first crossed my mind.

The flicker of her eyes

sparked the wick afire,
and all was play until the base of the flame
pressed its full weight on the tip of the candlestick:

wax dripped warm down the stem, beading sweat on her brow;
cascading tresses—translucent-peach in a waft of candlelight—
cleaved to her rounded back;

my hand on her delicate neck, an egg that swallows its yolk;
her bra neatly empty, strewn chaotically on the floor—
breasts soft to the touch, marionettes to every jerked-ripple
the fogged-glass chill elicited.

The sky clouded grey in her blue eyes as she looked at me,
all there was left of me was blue.
The wax dripped out of the bright hibiscus flower
blooming red, white, and gold at the tip of the curling wick.

My flesh, her flesh as one
individuality, its duality apparent
in the bright smile of her shadowed face.

I pulled away from the flame's perforating tickle,
lips soothed the burn still fluttering like a wing,
gently it succumbed to the puddled viscosity.
The scent of silent gasps melded with the smoke
crackling into our shared breath.

"Can you believe it?" she said
filled with the unabashed tenacity
of someone who's seen too much.
"Next year I might be pregnant."

Ultrasonic delirium overtook me as I envisioned
her flat stomach—a cat in full stretch—
engorging with the seed I wasted in youth
kindled into a being of worth,
something special, something human.

I lay naked, vulnerable, exhausted, shed:
how could something as brief as pleasure create life,
while destroying the notion of immortality?

My sepals, her bud, together would be me as I was,
a new person; and I would no longer be a version of myself
easily melted down and reshaped.

The life growing within her would solidify my own,
my life would abound in the shapelessness of its future.

No longer would I be a flickering light,
but a flame that burned bright until the wick exhausted the wax.

Whole

I've always wondered
why John Wesley Powell
decided to name the Colorado River
carving in Arizona a *canyon*
rather than chasm or gulch.
How easy it was then,
to name things that already had a name,

as the volatility and familiarity that coexist
like water and wine in your smile
which dimples closer to your nose than lips.
The fluoride stain on your upper, right front tooth—
a blemish you recently noticed
as you flossed the flesh gnawed off a plum pit,
and wanted to get rid of immediately—
is a water trickle
crying out of the sky,
that bleeds through the earth
slowly, boring its phantom body
into sedimented layers,
unaware of its gentle violence on its stubborn flesh
until what they form becomes something
greater than either,
belonging to neither.

The strength of your deodorant
surrenders to your sweat
by the time you get home;
it is the country song that comes on every time
you plug your phone into the car stereo—
a guilty pleasure to which I only know the beginning:
though I've heard it countless times in the last 6 years,
I wouldn't be able to hum its chorus.

I bear it while you put on your makeup—
using the visor mirror to save time—
in spite of not liking it,
not because its mystery is precious,
but simply because you say it makes you think of me.

Rather than feeling proud of having had
so many lovers before you, I feel sad
for each of them; for having put up with
a fragmented formation of me,
just how your phone always seems to live
at 3% even after you unplug
mine when I fall asleep
and you continue to live another life,
only to find its battery greet me
in the morning, agonizing red.

Sometimes it's easier to text
"ok" even when I'm angry at you—
my thumbs are bigger than the buttons,
smaller than the blocks of words
I'm trying to build into arguments—
because there's no other moment
when I feel the most love for you
than when I hate you.

In a similar way, I've wondered
why I use the things that irk me
about you to crutch my struggle
as I layer myself with me,
and we hide ourselves from us.

Why not allow the gaps between
what we want and what we'll never have
to be the things that hold us together,
instead of what marriage *really* is?

Calanques

There are depths unknown,
unexplored by our bodies.

Waters so blue, bluer than your eyes
when you're lost in one of your moods—

an island cliff whose face erodes, detached,
as rocks rifting from each other,

even when recovered from the sea
and reconciled, never can fit as they once were.

The pressure of the deep
takes your breath, steals your expectations,

steels you for the collapse
from the brunt, the mystery

that scares your protector—
a single breath, me in you.

I smile as we drown,
reciting iambs in your limbs,

sonnets coming from a sonofabitch
who hates it when you treat him

the way he treats you.
We frown and die

and decompose
yet live forever

in the droplets and air bubbles
that keep our bones from sinking.

Sur Place du Petit-Pont

Though the sky's lace veil
allowed the sun to peek
a smile through its crocheted dimples,
the clouds didn't withhold their rain.

The tour guide who advertised the ability
to reveal Notre Dame's secrets
stranded us under the hooves
of Charlemagne's horse
as we dripped in clothes that we washed
in the tub the night before
because our luggage was held captive
on a flight that never made it out of Los Angeles.

We skipped over soaked cobblestones,
four soles looking for sanctuary—
baptized in obsidian puddles—
at the feet of Our Lady's towering wooden doors.

A young *femme et mari*
posed in gown and tux
before a rose window,
trusting the evergreen of their joy
to the memory of a lens;
I smiled at the new lovers
because of where we were—
a city that had taken
Love as its *nom de plume*—
I remembered the sacred vows
we braided with something
so brittle as spoken words.

Then you kissed me
and didn't seem to mind
the waft of potatoes au Gratin
lingering from lunch,
the first-degree burn it seared
inside my mouth, still bleeding.

Yours tasted of iron—
the key ingredient in the prenatal
vitamins you started taking
in Marseille, the first place
we decided to start trying
for a baby, this time, for keeps—
you pursed your lips
into that wry smile you give me
whenever I forget which articles
of your clothes need to be hung
and which need to be machine-dried;

it reminded me of how you wrung
my ring finger with warm gold
in spite of the things
I didn't manage to fix
about myself by our wedding day,
or the flaws in you I continue
to ring like bells in a tower
even after we recited our own vows,
against our better judgment,
and I cried on the gown
you still haven't managed to resell.

These were the thoughts
flooding my mind the day
I saw the tower and spire
transfiguring over Paris,
burning bright as the day
we said goodbye to France,
floating away on the Seine.

Luceros

Our clothes slid from our skin
as did sun's shoulders into the sea.
We waded naked,
waist-deep and wrapped
by the warmth of stars
that floated through our tentacled fingers,
between our collective thighs

as fireflies carousing night's muggy breath.
I dipped my hand gently
as to not startle the droplets suckling
my skin cracks into its calm,

and took your womb like a water jug—
bone lined with mud soft as silt,
kilned by the afterday.

The black veil above us
obscured the liquid sloshing
in and out of your clay.
I took a deep swig of it—

thick, pungent clumps, briny in taste—
and continued to drink
until the blood that surrounded us—
which blotted from within you—
had been consumed.

Swaying its contours again through water,
the earthen ewer glowed as fire,
thirsty for star-nectar
that scuttled away in swarms.

The more light I captured with your lightness,
the darker the darkness
surrounding my pupils.
When I placed the womb
back in your body,

it turned night into day,
the water into milk,
and the stars into long ribbons
of wild mountain honey,
brown, as sweet and bitter as it was golden.

You combed its glimmer with your fingertips
as you unspooled a golden thread from your navel—
blonder than the blondest strand of your hair—
and crocheted a new soul with it,

one that would be *his:*
a new flame lit by a litany
sung in Magyar and Nahuatl—
sister tongues braided, burning as one.

Your solar plexus grew brighter and brighter—
as a red giant from a nebula—
beneath your full moon breasts
cratered thick of translucent milk veins

to nourish his defenselessness
into luminescence:
light from light,
true life from true life.

Nothing could've sparked his brilliance
as did the constellations
that swim in our bloods—
only light can make light.

Nothing would be able to extinguish it
as the stars in the sky
which were no longer there—
but were black and white pictures
taken millions of lifetimes before

when they lived and loved—
young, beautiful, celestial—
and stood before each other
as they never would again;
their echoes left behind like gossip
in the vast nothingness.

Super Mario Bros. Coin

We're the most common item
found in this two-bit overworld,
but as we warped down the ultrasonic tunnel black,
what I saw was a rather uncommon glow.

It was a life
too fragile still to keep,
strong in its ability to be there,
its inability to stay:

a cheep cheep resting
in water's deepest calm,
dreaming dreams I could
never dream of dreaming;

a grain of sand found
in the infinity of our oceans.
A memory, a fantasy, and a wish
latticed into a riddle:

how can an 8-bit cluster of achromatic pixels,
flickering 127 beats per minute—
a treasure glimmering as undeniably as gold—
make you feel more animal than human?

I squeezed your hand, as tight
as my mistrust of questions
that change depending on the answer,
and saw that same rare light in your eyes.

Moving Day

You are designer, yes?
the Russian mover mumbled
after I instructed him and his colleague
on where in the living room
they needed to place the skinny, espresso bookcase.

It was his way of relating to me
with the infinitesimal amount of English
he could muster without having
to ask me for reassurance.

His compliment was tinged
with the obligatory emasculation
that accompanies any conversation
amongst heterosexual men—

a disclosure that no hint
of vulnerability or kindness
will accidentally break out
under any circumstance.

A *je ne sais quoi* untaught
to all humans born with a penis
from a young age in order
to someday be allowed to claim

their manhood as if it were
a washer and dryer set
on 18-year layaway,
as when one of my friends

neared his boy's
one-year-old face to mine
not for me to kiss,
but for us to playfully butt heads.

I found the mover's
earnest attempt at emasculating
and insinuating a latent homosexuality in me
more endearing than offensive—

sweeter than when I learned
to masturbate in the 5th grade—
for being as honest as his tired
muscles and mandibles would allow him.

It was a natural impulse,
a duty that all self-respecting men
needed to detect and correct in one another
any deficiencies in testosterone,
by hazing those not man enough

to move their own homes,
and sought the armpit stench
and hairy butt-cracks of real men
hired to fulfill their spousal responsibilities,
satiating all of their ladies' needs—

from the bedroom to the kitchen,
bathroom and living room,
and move every back-breaking, unread book
she never had the heart to donate.

The only thing I flung over my shoulder—
past our new apartment's threshold
and the movers' scrotum-shriveling stares—
was the case meant to carry

the tennis racket my wife swung
backhanded in high school—
sharp and swift like a sword—
as if her maiden name rhymed
with Sharapova or Kournikova.

Now we use it to keep the dust
off the leftover rolls of Christmas wrapping paper—
a cornucopia stuffed with other things
we'd never deplete—because I had picked them out,
and she wouldn't want the people
receiving our gifts to think that we had bad taste.

The metal window box of succulents
I bought for her on Valentine's Day
hung defeated like a bronze medal
on the white balcony railing,
dead in their own soil.

All this unearthing and change and perspiration
so that I could see her body
filled with veggie pad thai and our unborn son;
she lay comfortable, wearing nothing
but the lingerie of shadows intermingled
with the afternoon light daggering through the blinds,

as she fell asleep—unfazed
by the coarseness of our naked mattress—
while I gently ripped the pillows and comforter free
from the trash bags we used
because we ran out of boxes.

The Opossum

Lying flat on cracked asphalt flesh—
perpetually in mourning
for those who lose their lives on its cheeks—
an opossum rested tranquil as leaves
that commend themselves to oneness with the road.

From its deep set eye-socket,
brimmed a melancholic compote
that dug its claws
into my sacrum holes
as I crossed a deserted
two-lane street onto the sidewalk,
skipping over scummy rainbow-oil puddles.

It was the glint in its eye—
bouncing streetlight as it cried—
that rippled in mine:
no matter how worthless
others might deem
your charred pelts to be—
when the best of you falls short
of anything anyone ever wanted—
it still hurts to die
knowing that no one cared.

An angel's spirit with Satan's teeth—
bone polished sharp,
stalactites and stalagmites
packed tight, void of might—
chalk marks of days counted down
to this Monday night
whose moon chose to
betray your crossing
as vulcanized rubber screeched

erratically, wedging the threads
you wear as nobly as a king's surcoat.

White fur waving freely
as the final whiskers of steam
rose from all the things you could've been—
your guts and blood, your oblation
waiting to be delivered
as melted snow on hollowed ground,
evaporated into smogged ether:
how many orphans did you
abandon shrieking in the night
without one to love them
as much as you did?

To say that I didn't see myself in you
would be a lie as false as the memory
of you as a pet who ran away
to form a family of its own,
in a land where people weren't cruel
and those who had mercy to give
gave it to those who needed it most,

and animals were respected
for the purpose they served
not the misconceptions
created by their appearance.
A world in which you'd make it
to the other side of the street—
on this very place—
to mourn the brown stain of me,
and the marsupial I loved,
burrowed in my cramped apartment
waiting for me, our rat baby

pouched warm in her womb.

Fellow traveler and jaywalker,
I'll remember you
as you were— a portrait
of an apostle's beard
minutes after martyrdom—
to be wiped away in the morning
as tears from a dream
you should've never woken from
as you hung upside down a tree
rooted in an upside down world—
dirt to my upside down rain—
fading into the darkest cave on earth:
a smile gripping to life.

In the Light of the Bas-Relief

—for Gio

Everything in the human body
was meant to perish, run out or break:
what do you expect?
God made it in one day—
on one of the last days of Creation—
and, unlike all of the amazing
abilities She gifted other animals,

She gave us the ability to believe,
to speak and name things as we saw fit,
and the ability to tell time—
not to know how much of it we have,
but that we have so little of it.

Yet I lie awake in disbelief
that you'll be as real as me—
lungs, heart, mind and soul
out of my cells as iron that rises
from the core, frozen as rock,
then molten, beaten and pressed,
reshaped into something useful in the home,
someone you'll grow to understand
as he shapes your habits
and you shape his nature
the way the Pacific swallows earth's crust
only to graft new land in the Atlantic.

And as I am only man,
not a wondrous beast or all-knowing god,
I will give you a name
that neither life, nor time, nor death
can ever take from you:
my son you will always be known as.

We were also given the best lips to kiss with,
and I will use them to kiss you all the kisses
that my time with you
will give me to kiss.

Cast as your father—
a role I chose in order to spare you from meeting
all of the men I pretended to be in my pasts—
we'll love our lives and learn
trust from our eternal mother, Time,
who always knows best
because She knows all
and will help you know *you.*

We'll enjoy Her fullness,
slow to unravel at first—
as sun warms us from within and without—
but is as fast and unexpected
as the names you'll give to the dawn and the dusk.

You'll think up things
I would've never thought of;
I'll stow them away in my thoughts
where you'll always live—
as when you were but a mere fantasy in my mind—
until I'm nothing more than a memory in yours.

In the Shadow of the Drowning Mammoth

Hours before her water broke,
my mind dwelled on the many ways
we could lose him—my boy, my son,
a tusk so deeply entrenched in me:
life's cruel limbo of making me love him
before giving him to me.

As I fell asleep,
I arrived at a park I'd visited once before,
desolate in the manner its dirt gripped my tombstone.
An old man approached me and took my hand;
as I looked down, I noticed that I too was old.
We walked toward a lake
alive with turtles, mosquitoes and tadpoles.

His wrinkles of cracked earth
seemed burdened with visions,
so I asked him how wisdom was acquired
as the stones we threw skipped flat
on the lake's tarry surface; he said:

"You acquire it as seconds
age a child from newborn to adult;
it compiles on your soul
as breaths in your lungs,
by the time you notice it's flowing into you,
you feel as though you don't have enough of it."

As we watched the awkward transition
of frogspawn from tadpole to froglet,
my thoughts asked what my words couldn't:
"Was I a good father?"
A question whose answer I didn't want to know.

The old man dipped his hands into the muddy waters,
and trapped a tadpole between his wrinkled palms.
He blew into his cupped hands
intoning melodies of amaranth, capri, and lilac.

"We're all born with light
and dark inside ourselves,"
he said, as he blew a new canticle with each breath.
"We need both, as light feeds on darkness
and darkness is renewed after it dies.
Everyone has some of both—
some of us more light
and some more dark than others."

When he opened his hands,
a golden frog jumped out
and into the lake, glowing bright
as it swam deep into the foggy depths.

"We all want more light than dark,
to succeed without failing,
do good and be told we are good,
to live forever and never die:
but don't crave more light; seek balance.
Don't allow others' darkness,
or the shadows wombed within you
to prey on your light;
pray on your light
that you may share it with those you love."

When I awoke, my wife's fountain
flowed warm from within,
and we drove to the hospital.
As stars and streetlights ushered our way,

the old man's words followed me
on Hollywood's empty, serene streets
as bats singing cassette tape squealings.

The lift of their wings
wrung my tear ducts,
and I wept the love saturating my bones
as the tar that consumed the mammoths
thousands of years before
only to preserve them forever.

The sun lay the moon to bed
as the wind soothed the clouds to sleep,
when the jacarandas polka-dotted the grass purple
and she told me that she couldn't wait to be a mother.

As she squeezed my hand tight,
I felt my heart tadpole
and mature into something
that wanted to leap
out of my rib cage and into my throat—
a golden aftertaste
of moments that make you
so happy that they make you sad
because you can't press pause
on a time that won't be like this again.

Ferning

—for Nicole

She asked me to stand by her side,
but I wanted to see it all
because I knew that I'd forget
even as hard as I'd want to remember:
the brunt and the bitter
forcing our son, our oneness, into the world.

My curiosity was stronger than her contractions,
as I saw *mi hijito's* soft skull—
draped in silty, mousy-brown hairs—
swirling inside of her
as an eyeball blinking her labia
open and shut and open again
for the first time,
our baby not quite ready to see
who was waiting for him
this side of his mother.

I had never seen her so vulnerable,
depleted, her joy at the cusp of life,
yet lodged so inconceivably deep,
nearly impossible to push out
in spite of all her might;
all the night without peace,
what little time had passed between breaths,
and was yet to come in the immediate unknown.

We were approaching a forest
where the air was rarefied,
our vows ratified,
we held our breath
and pushed—each time more unbearable.
Her legs, wide as hours spread by the second,

his unheard cries just a few minutes away
from never, from disbelief.

A constellation of nurses
descended from every corner
of the hospital and hovered over
her pain, nausea and my sobbing
as angels over a Petri dish of strange,
single-souled bacteria reproducing before their eyes.

The waft of her sweet iced breath, urine ammonia,
and pungent waste rushing out of anywhere it could,
reminded me that a relationship
was a scrapbook of hardships
collected, cut and pasted
onto pages that you flipped years later
to relive the momentary happiness
you missed while you were busy
looking on the road for the right things
to put in your pocket.

The path to our new home
revealed itself as the doctor
accidentally flicked the thick,
uterine blood onto my sweat rancid shirt.

Although the doctor sutured her tears,
taking her time to reshape
the gateway to pleasure and life—
that which was no longer what it was
and what it never would be again—
as Michelangelo chiseled David's buttocks
to approximate a perfection never seen before,

I was left with a gaping hole in my chest,
one that saturated itself full with healing
when his warm defenselessness lay on mine:
all the wounds they closed on her opened in me,
all the things they took out of her were placed in me.

She lay defeated,
deflated, our child—
our blood swaddled in her blood—
beat on her engorged, leaking chest
like a heart outside the body;
a thing she'd love like nothing before,
a love that would end only in death.

As we breathed for three,
I breathed for two more—
my unborn older brother
and my lost baby.

In the midst of my joy,
I mourned all the things Nicole lost
on our way to this moment
as the deceased purge their corpse of a soul:
her placenta, the ability to walk,
her blood and the drops of amniotic fluid
shed from her body in our bedroom,
the car and my shoes.

The doctor collected a sample of it
when we first arrived at the hospital
and slid the drops under a microscope:
"It's called ferning," she said, inviting us to see,
"because the salt crystals look like fern leaves."

About the Author

José Luís Oseguera is an LA-based writer of poetry, short fiction and literary nonfiction. He has published over 100 pieces of literature in over 60 publications including *Emrys Journal, The McNeese Review,* and *The Main Street Rag.* His work has also been nominated for the 'Best of the Net' award (2018 and 2019) as well as the 'Pushcart Prize' (2018 and twice in 2019). *The Milk of Your Blood* is his first poetry collection.

www.ingramcontent.com/pod-product-compliance
Lightning Source LLC
Chambersburg PA
CBHW022014080426
42733CB00007B/603